Basecamp

The Smarter, Faster, and Easier Way to Manage a Successful Podcast

by James Martell

Clearbrook Web Services Inc.
1415 Maple Street
White Rock BC Canada
V4B 5C5

www.podcastingmastery.com
helpdesk@podcastingmastery.com

DISCLAIMER

This booklet has been written to provide information about managing a successful podcast. Every effort has been taken to make this booklet as complete, helpful and accurate as possible.

This booklet is intended to be educational and instructional. The author and/or the publisher do not guarantee that the information contained in this workbook is comprehensive or complete, and will not be responsible for any errors or omissions. The author and/or publisher bear neither liability nor responsibility to any person or entity with respect to any loss or damage caused or alleged to be caused directly or indirectly by the information in this booklet.

TABLE OF CONTENTS

INTRODUCTION

Would you like to learn about a tool I use that allows me to manage my podcasting business with ease and achieve long term success in an industry where most people burn out quickly?

Hi, my name is James Martell and I'm the host of the popular *Podcasting Mastery* podcast, broadcast weekly from the **Secret Beach Hut Studio**. I've been podcasting for 13 years and over that time I've learned the secrets of how to create a stress-free lifestyle business.

To me, there are many advantages to developing a lifestyle business, and if you do it the right way you will spend less time *actually* doing business, more time *enjoying* your family, more time *travelling*, and more time doing "all of the things" that matter to *you* most.

You can do this by focusing on strategies that develop both passive monthly income streams, and passive ways of developing new clients and customers for your business.

So, with this in mind, let me introduce you to this booklet: *Basecamp - The Smarter, Faster, and Easier Way to Manage a Successful Podcast.*

Now, you probably know me as the host of **Podcasting Mastery**, but what you may or may not be aware of is that I am also the host of the **Affiliate Buzz**, the **first** and **longest** running podcast in the affiliate marketing industry!

We just released our **430th episode** and celebrated our **13th** anniversary for the show, and one of the things I am most proud of is our consistency in the publication of the ongoing episodes.

In 13 years, I have missed only one episode per year on average!

I credit this consistency to an associate of mine, Charles Johnston, who put a system in place for me early on, which has made it very easy for me to produce episodes in less than an hour.

This system has obviously evolved over the years, and I want to share it with you because, quite frankly, there's a fair bit of information online about **"how to start a podcast"**, but what's missing is information on **"how to successfully manage a podcast over time."**

Believe me, there's a big difference between the two!

MP3 AUDIO INTERVIEW

Basecamp – The Smarter, Faster, Easier Way
to Manage a Successful Podcast

Listen here:

http://podcastingmastery.com/basecamp360/

Password: basecamp360

CHAPTER 1: THE REASONS WHY SO MANY PODCASTS DON'T LAST AND HOW BASECAMP IS A GAME-CHANGER

It's one thing to launch your show, but it's a *whole* other thing to manage it on an ongoing basis, which is another reason why the average podcaster fades away after ONLY their seventh episode.

Known in the podcasting industry as "PODFADE", this happens for basically two reasons:

1. Underestimating the workload: The podcaster dramatically underestimates the workload required to manage a successful podcast, and they attempt to do everything themselves: audio editing, show notes, graphics, finding guests, conducting the interview, promotion . . . everything, and they get overloaded and overwhelmed.

In my book, *Outsourcing Essentials for Podcasters - The Secrets to Hiring Talent on a Beach Hut Budget (available at Amazon)*, I share the exact steps I use to hire a low-cost virtual team (audio editor, writer, graphic designer, and – most important – a personal virtual assistant), to support YOU in your podcasting efforts.

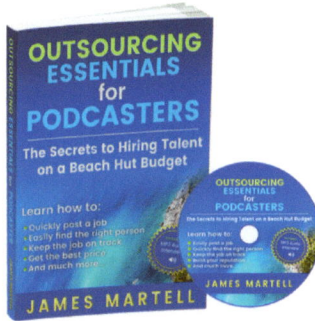

2. Lack of a System: The podcaster does not have a system in place for the development and production of their ongoing episodes, or the management of their virtual team and promotion of individual episodes, resulting in sporadic publication or the dreaded **PODFADE**.

I don't want this to happen to you.

Instead, imagine having a smarter, faster, and easier way to manage your podcast – where you can get everything you need to do in less than 60 minutes per episode, and where your virtual team takes care of everything else like clockwork, including:

- Finding, contacting and coordinating your guests
- Preparation of your episode outlines
- Editing the audio for each episode
- Development of SEO-friendly show notes
- Publication of the episode on your website

- Confirmation that all the podcast directories have the latest edition
- Promotion of the episode on Facebook, Twitter, LinkedIn and YouTube
- Distribution of the episode to all email subscribers
- All of the little things that need to be done for you to be successful

And all this is wrapped up in a simple, easy-to-use, online project management system called **Basecamp.** It will give you to get everything done that you need to do in less than 60 minutes per episode, and where (again) your virtual team takes care of everything else in a well-managed and predictable way.

CHAPTER 2: MY STORY AND EXPERIENCE WITH BASECAMP

Prior to using Basecamp, I was finding it extremely difficult to manage my podcasting business.

I was very busy, having 10-15 projects on the go at any one time. I had so many things to juggle and issues to sort out such as:

- website development, SEO services, podcasting services
- managing a team of writers, graphic designers, techies, editors
- team members a different locations
- files in different places (images, documents)
- versioning issues (who has the most recent version of)

My team and I were overwhelmed.

We had frequent ". . . *where the heck are we at?"* meetings.

We had projects in various stages of completion.

It was difficult to stay organized.

Moral was down; team members were fighting.

I was grumpy from sleepless nights.

We were dropping the ball for clients.

Out of pure frustration one evening, I searched Google for online project management systems. I'd looked at others in the past, but they were complicated – way overkill for what we needed.

Out of pure luck, I stumbled across Basecamp and it looked very promising, offering a 60-day, no-obligation free trial – you didn't even have to give credit card details!

So I set-up an account, watched a few 1-minute video tutorials, added a project, and then started inviting the team and within a few days we were using Basecamp to manage our projects.

And suddenly I found that:

- The *"...where the heck are we at?"* meetings faded away.
- Everybody became far more productive, which meant more profitable for me.
- The team was happier.
- I was MUCH happier.

And then, naturally, I then started using Basecamp to manage my podcast . . . and BINGO!

Basecamp was the perfect solution for managing a podcast, and I will say since I found Basecamp we have used it successfully to manage **over 150 projects!**

It's amazing!

I have recommended Basecamp to individuals managing small businesses to mid-size corporations (and of course podcasters) and we all agree that *"we would not know what we would do without Basecamp because it makes our lives so much easier."*

CHAPTER 3: GETTING YOUR VIRTUAL TEAM ONBOARD

Now, before we talk about the **6 key features of Basecamp** that are going to make your podcasting life so much easier, let me talk about your members first, and how they relate to Basecamp. Of course in my booklet, *Outsourcing Essentials for Podcasters - The Secrets to Hiring Talent on a Beach Hut Budget*, I cover hiring and working with your virtual team members in great detail.

If you haven't reviewed that book and the companion audio, I would encourage you to do so. In it I teach you how to hire a writer, audio editor, graphic designer, or techie and (most importantly) a personal virtual assistant.

I promise you, you'll be pleasantly surprised how absolutely *inexpensive* these freelancers are, and when you see it, you'll quickly realize you'd be crazy to do these tasks yourself, when you can have experts at your fingertips to take care of things for you, in a very, very professional way.

So, back to *Basecamp*.

Once you have set-up a free trial account (again - no credit card required), you can set-up the Basecamp for your podcast, and once that's done, you can click on the "Invite More People" link at the top of the page in Basecamp, and then enter the email address for each of your team members. They will then receive an email inviting them to join you within the system.

I'll point out as well, that their email address is the same email address that your team members will receive alerts from Basecamp from, as tasks are assigned to them by you and others working on your podcast.

CHAPTER 4: THE 6 KEY FEATURES OF BASECAMP

I want to delve into the **6 key features of Basecamp** that are going to make the management of your ongoing podcast episodes so much easier.

These 6 key features include:

1. Discussions
2. To-Dos
3. Files
4. Text Documents
5. Events
6. Progress

1. DISCUSSIONS

In Basecamp you can set-up a Discussion between team members, and one of the things I do is set up an individual Discussion for each podcast episode that I create. A Discussion is perfect for managing your episodes and your team.

Let me walk you through an example scenario . . .

Let's assume you have a Virtual Assistant, and they are organizing and managing the interview. They have already confirmed the attendance of your Writer and Audio Editor, and both are onboard with the Basecamp system.

Step 1: *Post a New Discussion* – Your Virtual Assistant would post a "New Discussion" in Basecamp and give it a name (I.e. Episode #033 - John Smith, and the name of the topic covered).

Step 2: *Add Episode Outline Template* – Your Virtual Assistant adds an episode outline template to that Discussion, and fills in the guest introduction, bio and adds the questions and a call to action.

Step 3: *Invite Host to Discussion* – Your Virtual Assistant then invites you to the discussion, simply by posting a little note down at the bottom of the Discussion, selecting a checkbox beside your name, and hitting submit. You will then receive an email with a link back directly to this Discussion in Basecamp.

Step 4: *Make Adjustments to Episode Outline* - Host (you) make any changes, additions or modifications to the episode outline until you are happy with it.

Step 5*: Conduct Internet* - Host (you) uses the episode outline to conduct the interview.

Step 6: *Upload Raw Audio File* – Your Virtual Assistant adds a comment and uploads the raw audio file for the episode to this same discussion and shares it with your Writer and Audio Editor.

Step 7: *Upload Show Notes* – Your Writer adds a comment and uploads the completed show notes for the episode to this same discussion and shares it with your Virtual Assistant.

Step 8: *Upload Audio File* - Audio Editor add s a comment and uploads the completed audio file for the episode to this same discussion and shares it with your Virtual Assistant.

Step 9: *Publish Episode to Website* - Virtual Assistant add and publish the completed show notes and audio file for the episode to your website.

Step 10: *Promote Episode* - Your Virtual Assistant promotes the episode.

The bottom line is the Basecamp functionality for a Discussion is perfectly-suited to managing each of your individual podcast episodes.

> *TIP: Once you have completed the episode you can archive the episode within the Basecamp system. If you need to refer to it at a later date you will have your episode outline, show notes, raw and edited audio file, and the notes on where and how the episode was promoted.*

2. TO-DO LISTS

I am sure we all know what a to-do list is. The main feature here is you can set-up multiple "to-do lists" to help you stay organized, and within each "to-do list" you can add multiple to-dos.

You can also assign each "to-do" to a team member and assign a date for when the to-do needs to be completed by – for example, let's say you wanted to create a promotional image for a particular episode.

Step 1: You (or your Virtual Assistant) would click on Post a "New To-Do List" and give it a name (I.e. Promotional Image for Episode #042). That's the name of the to-do list.

Step 2: You would then add a series of to-dos and assign the appropriate team member to each, and then assign a date for when the to-do needs to be completed by. You might add a "to-do" to the "to-do list", such as:

- for your writer to write the text you would like included on the image
- for your graphic designer to create the image
- for your virtual assistant to add it to the website
- for your virtual assistant promote it on Facebook

3. FILES

This is a great feature because all of your "files" for podcast are in one place – similar to Dropbox, but on steroids, because these "files" (images, audio files, documents) can **ALL** be attached to discussions, to-dos, and text documents were they are easy to find.

One of the **BIG** challenges I have found managing "files" online email, is keeping track of them. They are typically on my desktop computer, laptop, tablet, in my email, on my phone, in Skype, on other people's computers, in their email . . . pretty much all over the place.

The solution is Basecamp.

All of the files for the podcast go into Basecamp: the show artwork (and all the various sizes), logos, and the audio files for each of the episodes, and promotional materials (i.e. Facebook images, free PDF reports, etc.). That way I know where they are, and the team members can find them when they need them.

It's an ideal solution that solves a **BIG** time waster – which is looking for missing files.

4. TEXT DOCUMENTS

This is another great feature. This is where you can create and store text documents. I use it as the perfect place to store all of our procedures. These might be the full step-by-step procedures for my Virtual Assistant to promote each podcast episodes.

I have all of the procedures stores here for the Graphic Designer to create the show artwork, or the Audio Editor to edit the most recent episode, and all 30+ procedures that the team uses to manage the podcast, so quite frankly, I don't have to.

And just like the Discussions, To-Do Lists and the Files, they can all be easily shared with other Team Members by adding a comment below the actual Text Document for them, then selecting their name from the list that appears and then clicking submit. They will then **INSTANTLY** receive an email from Basecamp alerting them to the document you just shared with them.

5. EVENTS

This is a wonderful feature. In Basecamp there is an internal calendar, which you can use to set-up, schedule and invite members to an event.

For example, if you were going to record a podcast on Thursday at 2:00 Pacific Time:

Step 1: You (or your Virtual Assistant) would click on "Events" in the Upper Menu, then select the Date, then give the Event a name (I.e. Record the Affiliate Buzz), and then select the time.

Step 2: You would then add any Notes, and then invite participating team members, add a reminder and then click on Add this Event. Now everybody has been alerted by email, and a reminder email has been queued for them.

6. PROGRESS

I love this feature. The Progress area of Basecamp is brilliant, because with one click, you can see exactly what's been happening in your projects on a day-by-day basis.

It lets you stay right up-to-date on everything that's going on. Do you remember the *"...where are we at meetings"* I mentioned earlier where we were overwhelmed? This use to happen because I was not sure where we were at with projects that were in various stages of completion.

I was having difficulty staying on top of things, which lead to sleepless nights . . . The Basecamp Progress feature solves all this. I now know at a glance, exactly where we are at with the projects. I can see all of the messages that were updated, completed a to-do, comments, files uploaded everything I need to see to know where I am at.

Basecamp is amazing!

CHAPTER 5: BASECAMP AND YOUR BUSINESS

So, again the **6 key features in Basecamp** include:

- Discussions
- To-Dos
- Files
- Text Documents
- Events
- Progress

I encourage you once you get logged into Basecamp, to have a good look around.

Make yourself at home, I'll bet you are going to love Basecamp, and you will be like the rest of us in no time, *"wondering how in the heck you ever lived without it!"*

I will also bet once you get your podcast organized and set-up in Basecamp, you will expand its use and add additional projects for other aspects of your business.

It really is that good!

BASECAMP TUTORIALS

I would also recommend watching the Basecamp video tutorials, and have each of your team members do the same. The video tutorials are very short, easy-to-follow and will quickly get you, and your team orientated to this amazing productivity tool.

Dig in, and before you know it you will have a smarter, faster, and easier way to manage your podcast – and where you can get everything you need to do in less than 60-minutes per episode, and where your virtual team takes care of everything else in a well-managed and predictable way.

ADOPTING BASECAMP

I have found that most team members easily adopt Basecamp without any push back. This was quite surprising. I had assumed many would be resistant to change.

This biggest thing I had to deal with is just a few habits. We were all used to sending files in an email. They would say, "I'll send the file to you in an email as an attachment". And I would have to say "no, please add it to Basecamp", and they would go "Oh, okay, of course".

I have also found when hiring a freelancers from Upwork, many are already very familiar with Basecamp. This makes things simple.

I have also found that most freelancers who are not familiar with Basecamp, adopt it quickly. This is a good thing.

There are of course those who are resistant to using Basecamp and push back. I am rigid though, and do not offer them a choice. If they decline or push back, I replace the freelancer.

It's that important that they embrace Basecamp.

CHAPTER 6: IS BASECAMP DIFFICULT TO SET-UP?

In a word **"No"**. The one challenge however, is many podcasters do not have a set of written procedures for all of the tasks that need to be accomplished to manage and grow a successful podcast.

This is where my *Podcasting Mastery* course really shines, because I include all of our fill-in-the-blanks templates and worksheets, our project descriptions and work orders, and all of the step-by-step procedures necessary to manage a successful podcast.

This is *the same internal collateral we use* to manage my podcasts, and podcasts for our clients.

Let me give you an example, because in addition to a **300+ page** *Podcasting Mastery* training manual and video series – where I teach the **8-steps** for creating a profitable podcast (one that not only YOU will be proud of, but one that will impress ALL who hear it) – students also receive all of our internal collateral including: fill-in-the-blanks templates and worksheets, our project descriptions and work orders and all of the step-by-step procedures, so you can do ALL of the work yourself. Or you can hand it off to your Virtual Assistant to do the work for you!

This is the same collateral I give to *my* Virtual Assistant, and the same collateral *my* Virtual Assistant gives to our graphic designer, writer, audio editor and so on. You can use these to do the work yourself, or to have your Virtual Assistant do and oversee the work for you.

You can find more information about *Podcasting Mastery - The 8 Steps You MUST Follow to Succeed as a Podcaster on the Internet* at www.podcastingmastery.com/course/

So there we have it: *Basecamp - The Smarter, Faster, and Easier Way to Manage a Successful Podcast.* I hope you found this booklet helpful and I'm sure the advice I have given you will allow you to manage your podcast with less stress and more success as you develop it into the ultimate lifestyle business.

Email: helpdesk@podcastingmastery.com
Telephone: (604) 542-0747

Website: www.podcastingmastery.com
Course: www.podcastingmastery.com/course/

www.ingramcontent.com/pod-product-compliance
Lightning Source LLC
Chambersburg PA
CBHW041756050426
42443CB00023B/16